PORTUGUESE SAILOR BOY

DAVID
APPELBAUM

PORTUGUESE
SAILOR BOY

 EYEWEAR PUBLISHING

First published in 2020
by The Black Spring Press Group
Suite 333, 19-21 Crawford Street
Marylebone, London W1H 1PJ
United Kingdom

Cover design and typeset by Edwin Smet
Author photograph by Kate Hamilton
Cover photograph by Wikipedia Commons

The right of David Appelbaum to be identified as author of
this work has been asserted in accordance with section 77
of the Copyright, Designs and Patents Act 1988

ISBN 978-1-913606-03-9

The editor has generally followed American spelling and punctuation at the author's request.

WWW.EYEWEARPUBLISHING.COM

For Pauline

David Appelbaum is Professor Emeritus of
Philosophy at SUNY, New Paltz. He is the
author of many books, including *Jacques Derrida's
Ghost: A Conjuration* and *The Delay of the Heart*.
He is a graduate of Harvard, past senior editor at
Parabola, and founder of Codhill Press.
His recent collections include *Notes
On Water: An Aqueous Phenomenology*
(Monkfish, 2018), among others.

TABLE OF CONTENTS

Never trust a Portuguese.
– old Irish proverb

LEGEND

We were one. We were many.
A fleet, an armada, a school of cod fishers
dispatched in a storm leagues thick.
The sun came to stillness at midday
our shadows in flight with dragonflies on the screen mesh.
Did we mean to go in haste?
Were we pilgrims or colony of the life-force borne forward?
Were we leaving or turning back for the remainder?
Our wants were minimal.
The log told cost and what had been,
although the mate was untrustworthy.
Many decried the journey's length which was prolonged.
Although we seemed steering along a narrow precipice
the coins dropt into the abyss were not ours
but the ship's phantasm, a ghost crew dreamt each night
with more claim to reality than we the sleepers.
Da Gamma's palm was a running sore, his hand obliged
to remain chained to the helm in raging seas.
The map, our home, an exact replica, complete with mermaids.
Only at the worn edges showing coastline.
We disputed coordinates, each a question
whether sketch of Ethiopia, stray shipping lane,
or code for secret orders.
We could deny the course but not change it.
The plot was set, to preclude a lengthy consensus.
Still, our arguments held endless council
in chapel, station, mess hall, bunk.
The school to which we were gifted was a transcendent word
that the cook placed on the tip of the scullery boy's tongue.
We kept to ourselves, though when the seas were high
collaboration was needed, even if relations were
met with contempt by the Marranos, ourselves.

Each day sank, an anchor at dusk to commence
nightly purgatory, when forward advance was held at bay.
Thus our condition, rich in provisions our lord had supplied,
poor in the same, sufficient to serve none but the fleetest
for fleet we were, whosoever were we.

CONVERSION

A bus will come. You mustn't not see to it. There will
be souls who don't know you. What you feel will be
called fear. It was so. In shambles of front yards, children
played, a new game for each house. You too are a child,
different from others, held in by a membrane not unlike
one that held us, dear brother, clasped in an amniotic
sea. When it arrived, a woman took my hand and had
me wait locked in a room for hours and days. I endlessly
cried my indignation. Outside, birdsong. I couldn't
stop the rattle in my chest. A voice said I was ashamed.
It was only a game we had called pirates. My job was
conquistador and to chase the rest, sparing no one. My
stick sword waved in the air like a winnowing cane. One
eye, I remember, was patched with a bloody bandage
and hurt from another fight. The thin woman with
blue hair, my tormentor, was unmoved by a confession,
which I made on the spot. She took me to a water
fountain for my dry heaves. Afterwards I was told that
something broken in me was fixed, but her words were
not reassuring. The opposite felt true.

LIFE WITHIN

CONVERSION

The ark on which we were borne, endowed by several
families who lived hierarchically, was snub-nosed,
like a dory, its empty hold slunk low in the water,
yet, apparently, no lower with all aboard, provisions
added. Once a slave galley, it had carried Barabbas to
his crucifixion with our master. We felt a shiver of
the incarnation upon boarding. Some said its sin of
transport was ingrained in the caulking. Different levels
represented specific questions, down to the lowest
where there was scarcely a breath of air. There the grand
inquisition was, *What is God?* To hear was difficult, the
waves cracked so near. It was known only by the cook's
boy who slept alone on the rock ballast. No one knew
his thoughts or whether he had any since he lacked
speech.

EVERY BEGINNING HAS A STORY

There was a sky ashen-lit like a screen.
A holly tree sketched a giant crab.
It was easy to forget it wasn't by the ocean.

Its pincers played against the windowpane
begging and giving, begging and giving –
the prey no different from the prayer.

Wake you, the dark will swallow,
like Jonah, in the fish's belly,
a lullaby my grandmother cooed,
a young-boy shadow by the petrified claw.

To where a body falls when light is gone?

I imagined birds migrating by night
heeding in them her song as she swept –
language once known, now forbidden:
Salt, breath dying, I forgive my love.

Her voice, weft to wind, bellows
impotence at the storm, lowering
the pitch to better shatter glass.
Holly leaves scatter like sand.

Rough planks, sea-worn from rain
stained with mollusk, curl at the edges
as if the adze had been too dull
to dovetail a hull together.

Dark hickory, caulked with mud,
maps the plunder in small markings
as if the portion astern remained
only in the minds of the brigands.

THE PHONE CALL

A windstorm had taken the power down.
The upstairs phone rang and rang.
It didn't stop when I picked it up.
The voice inside was my grandmother's.
Don't go, I want you should know.

Yingle. She was young again. *Yingle,*
these years I've been dead, shame left
me silent. Soft ring-tone tears
fell from the receiver's mouth,
barely dammed by the breathing holes.

Tell me, is love such a good thing
when it comes home to crush you?
She sat on a squat Turkish ottoman,
assumed a posture of supplication.

A big-bead African necklace coiled
around her throat like a fat phone cord.
With a pearl cigarette holder she smoked
like a flapper girl in a Camels ad.

I forget what he would call himself,
second jazz trumpet from the local club.
Her gravel voice syncopated the vowels.
The devil he was when he held me.

Rain found its way back, thunder pealed.
She pressed my head to her silk blouse.
The scent, rose water and tobacco, calmed,
like the graininess of old leather.

These peccadilloes bite our ankles like fleas.
She hummed a lullaby in Russian.
They have a special warning
like those brown spots on your hands.

Horns wailed, I thought, in the downspout.
Whole cities crumbled in their wake.
My grandmother danced like a houri,
probably some version of the Charleston.

Yingle, she said, *they come to stone me*.
Her wheelchair was wide for the aisle.
You must help uphold my dignity.
You must swear witness to the truth.

Innocence holds no charm against evil.
My life is an unclean mess, *tref*.
Surely a heart's desire extenuates.
The local library has the law journals.

She pressed two salty fingers to my lips.
Though an artist you still have brains.
With you, I have such hope, she said.
Es bricht mir fast das Herz.

Those years you spent happy in Berlin
as if no one else had their troubles.
I had boarders to take in.
Your father went on the warship.

The great hall of the Zurich Opera House,
they were performing *Carmen* in German.
The toreadors wore SS uniforms
and sang arias consistently off-key.

Was work so hard looking for you?
But forgive, each to his own *mishegas*.
The past you must repair, she was saying.
Sew it together, wax the stitches sealed.

Fringes of wig turned her face into a rose,
(maybe I was confused with her name)
before my mind could present a case,
the phone went dead, or the dream.

Not a thing she'd said stayed with me.

WORKSTATION

I once had a supervisor, a gaunt man.
He gave make-work, piles of it.
At closing time one day he stood nearby
to say without ceremony he was leaving.

He made no attempt to hide anguish.
The desk, legendary among us, lay in shambles
a free association of receipts due and
a future hinged on neglects of his station.

No one was permitted near the holy heap.
He displayed an uncanny knack, on command,
to retrieve a slip of memorandum or
personal letter re: account X in an instant.

He wasn't evil – unless dispassion was –
but the opposite of self-effacing.
That was why tears in his wine-red eyes
were a difficult call for empathy.

He said he had served his role well,
that our enterprise deserved new blood.
Now graying ideals once animate in youth
were unable to lead him elsewhere.

One had to arm for inevitabilities
to let old appreciations flail
to separate the chaff from the seed.
A leather brief hung slackly in his grip,

an awkward pause just over my desk.
My father, his wedding suit laid each night
folded and starched, an iron chair by his bed:
each day he told it was for the coffin.

The supervisor brooded over that fate.
My head lowered in a modicum of respect
as the key turned in the door a last time –
he went off to serve an errant justice.

THE PORTOLAN

That I desired travel so late in life
took hold as a delicious mystery.
How pleasant to imagine Vasco de Gama
was my grandfather's great-great-grandfather.

In its folds, the map was a memory.

Before my eyes, ornate shields crossed
to signify how clans divided the pastel surf.

As friends said, it came to me reluctantly
that the coastline was less fretted than earlier,
certain ports of call had ceased owning a mark,
falling away like ravished dunes.

The scrape of boots along the shore, beheld
by a score of eyes from a musty deck
or of such who pertained to it and lost or lost
and pertained to it in loss:
all a great lesson for me, map-reading
sea-swells on the precipice of my bed.

Scrolls of legends furrowed its brain
while the cerulean water plunged
the ship on a southerly to Madagascar.

Its poop glass reflected the young yellow sun.
I read the strange script, Greek or Hebrew
whose tongue-tying fricatives clanged
like a buoy outside the last harbor.

According to legend, it was redrawn after
Balboa's 1513 journey to the South Sea
by one Pedro Ramel, inventor of rhumb lines
as commissioned by King Manuel I,
The Fortunate, Lord of Ethiopia, Arabia,
Persia, and India, rendered destitute
in body and soul in the pestilential wake
of the Plague that left bodies blackened.

Each wave, exquisitely drawn with quill
conveyed a singular portion of a life
that when held to lamplight was my own.
The veins were daubed in a faded blue,
somewhat like an anatomy lesson.

The primal scene was there, hapless child,
a thirst for joy, seasons, summer, winter,
storms to fray the heart's torn edges,
paradoxical calms, the night stars:
seeing how I always strayed apart
an olive branch adrift from land
subject to the whims of cartography
that eternally await a Noah to read it.

My cousin the painter told me
how laurel leaves fit the hero, a dunce cap
for one who denies the explorer's spirit.

Most ragged were the thin edges.
Where frayed, the wind blew parchment
to compete with the former shoreline.
The land thus littered with propositions.

The real couldn't be told from the mean.

As the eye reaches its limit (was it there?)
a Moorish warrior brandished his sabre
outside a fortified city by the Indian Ocean
while a bluish veil dulled a faraway castle.

From his caravel, Vasco saw the same
festoon of soldiers as they dragged
prisoners of war across blank dunes
toward a chamber of torture.
Bird cries filled the desert air
drowning the conquistadors' ribaldry
so that beauty, too, slouched toward Mecca.

To read the high quadrant of the map
took balance and skill. Perseverance won
on tiptoes until mercifully I fell
into a fevered dream of bold piracy
that would change everything.

It did not. The dream was recurrent.
It was the attainment that ran away.

THE WARTIME PARK

The fountain. The fountain.
I, a flying fish, mouth agape, skimming waves.
My father, back from combat, had no furlough.
He raced a ghost that tripped on headstones.

It was war. Park trees were pruned military-style.

An old man sat on one bench playing solitaire.
There was the joker, one-eyed Phoenician sailor.
Death by water, he vanished it before my eyes.

My thirst was a memory haunting.
It wasn't content with a feeble stream,
rationed by drought and allotted to the spigot.
Drink, my father said. His kidneys gave out.

I ran. A sudden downpour drowned the dust,
thickened the path to tropical muck.
To burrow into the brick fort was forbidden while
the near woods exploded in nitric light.

A face looked back under war paint.

Outside the womb, the east front collapsed,
imperilling the fragile beachhead.
The mirror stared back with my eyes. In
them an immediate future dimmed.

The fountain was dry. On the spigot
a sign hung like a dog tag on a steel chain. I
didn't know what the red letters said.
It was probably a word like poison.

The obstacle was a six-foot retaining wall.
The maps for assault didn't show
what the First Marines learned empirically.

The fog of war crept lynx-like
over the fallen first, then the dead standing.
Their images too were a stain
that revealed the desert by blinding.

They were neuter, thus absolved of blame.

It furthers one to cross the short strand.
The red fox loses its tail.
Nothing is left to drink.

MY AUNT'S ADVICE

Tante Faiga called late one night.
Her sister booked second-class on the *Lusitania*.
The day had more hours than needed.

I wasn't bored. I wasn't discontent.
I lay awake, occupied with maps.
Ocean depth fascinated the way
it drew tiny ciphers on wavy black lines.
It read like a fugue score.

How ballast makes a ship float, I imagine,
is most likely that gravity is devious,
down isn't toward the depressive
but a gap between where and there.

I was grown, high in the sheet music business.
It was a malaise that my artist friends
came to lunch with me out of sympathy.

After all, my sole claim to honest fame
was knowing how deep the ocean is,
how far down the Bermuda Triangle goes –
where the Ural Mountains drop undersea,
whether a submarine desert ever blooms.

My painter friend set me for dinner.
This was after a big Klee exhibition.
He stands pat, he observed, like geometry.
All play and less than no work.

Whole cities are underwater, I said.
Atlantis, but also Orca and Mezith.
Souls there must be some amphibian species
taking in oxygen with lacy gills.

My mother lives below, alone with fish.
Easy it isn't to be a companion,
but remember, caves and vaults within
the heart are also undersea things.

Dreams, he thought, should move between
since they too arise from water
since they expire, brought to the surface.
He said one ought to take diving lessons
to do innovative work with oil paint.

The tab arrived in a black envelope.
It looked like an undertaker's invoice.
We lingered on the deck over the harbour where whales
were spotted the week before.

In valediction he said, I'm painting a *Pietá*.
The torso is drawn with pure ultramarine.
Such impulses express grave inner doubt
as I have no belief in the afterlife.

The walk home was pouring rain.
The streets alive with tiny frogs.
Thousands had seized the moment to live.
My shoes kept slipping on them off the berm.

Their staccato gave a subliminal pulse
that must have had a secret action.
I stopped somewhere for a nightcap
remembering my aunt's words,
No choice if no resolve.

On a used napkin I composed a song.
The refrain went, *This flow. Why sadness?*
It sold. I was not unhappy.

DUTCH TREAT

On the train from Hoek van Holland
to Calais, an old man handed me a cigar.
Cuban, he said. I imagined pineapples
and banana trees and war-torn bays.

The cabin was hot, the air blue.
He wore a wool suit and smoked impressively.
During the war, he said, I went with torches.
They were to illumine the four corners.

You had ten minutes to get the plane down,
another ten to get the guns off.
These were cow fields; mind you,
you never knew where you were stepping.

One dark night, my foot found a hole.
I fell like a casualty onto the wet grass
into a fox burrow with pups newly-whelped.
Their acid tongues licked my face.
It was like having my soul peeled off.

The mother was gone. Imprinted, I
took and nursed and reared them.
The pack worshipped me as a god.
My fingers grew crafty at trapping mice.

The animal heart isn't so different
from the human. In this way we grew close.
I became more wild and they tender,
housepets sleek in fox-fur coats.

To say what nature of rapport,
the several seemed to read my desire
which would lead to strange places.
Once they uncovered a German camp.

The brood set off the din of Athens' geese.
The Maquis were able to rout them
before they dove into the trenches.
I then knew the blood lust of the Valkyries.

Nature must take her course.
Even what war was was winding down.
The foxes were full-sized vixens
as we snuck to deploy the lights.

It was the largest I called Churchill
who bit my hand with quiet relish.
It was the law. I saw she was grown
lusting after blood due the Alpha.

The train was passing Flemish country
fields of poppy, rows of crosses.
My host took out a fresh cigar.
I was once a fox, he craftily said.

His blue eyes took on a feral look.
(It might have been the smoke.)
The purity of the animal soul, he said,
remains virginal, no thick tongue of fear.

Warm fur smell of briar
a jewel of the moon to bay at:
but I was a man, human, all too human,
a brain once addled by the hunt.

To disembark he rose, the courts at Bruges.
As one palm balanced the valise,
the scar there, perfect stigmata.

LATIN

The word is a fishbone in my throat
millennia after Roman soldiers
phalanx after bronzed phalanx
marched across San Marco.
After which I was named.

Below my mahogany window seat
a beggar, a leper stands naked
beneath the walls of Jerusalem
under sun, alms lie unused in a bowl
while he chants prayers of the Hebrews.

Vercingetorix
whose assault re-occupied the hill
where four thousand men died
like rams slaughtered for feast day,
your spies having drugged them
sweet wine laced with antimony.

I couldn't say the name.
Splinters pierced my tongue.
Northrup, the Latin teacher,
would rap the back of your hand.
One night he slashed his wrists
with a kitchen knife, a family heirloom.

He was a phthisic man, elfish,
thin as a diphthong.
Sirens rent the village sleep.
The town doctor, my father, went on call.

Grave after grave filled
with Etruscans, kith and kin to Rome,
my father's too, after his car swerved –
he'd been trained in Florence
and grew to appreciate the irony
of gentle Fra Angelico's art.

Latin names of joint and limb,
A dead language for dead things, he said.
Italian schools aren't good at anatomy.
The autopsy was unsure which artery burst.
One's heart is rich with choice.

Vercingetorix, no *homme gallant*
whose loves predate mortal sin
but boys with tongues too thick
for pursed lips to say *we hate you*.

Death rejected its teacher of declension.
Northrup recited Roman exploits for years.
Pupils left to think the word for luck
was the Latin my father got wrong.

THE ARRIVAL

My cousin the doctor arrived in a Piper Cub.
On the runway he pushed it with one hand.
The wonder of super-light design.
An Air Force jumpsuit had him look an ace.

He liked to navigate the night sky.
He learned this skill, he said, in Russia.
Surveys were rewarded with rock formations
from which seeped the earth's black milk.
Geology, he said, was his new god.

An impromptu meal appeared on the table.
Her wake would be with grace and song.
After, we found stairs to the garden.
Over the stucco wall, thyme ran wild.

His sister had children with different men.
Their looks took after the husbands.
The youngest insisted on a helmet
with bug-eyed lenses for night vision.

She had opinions on an afterlife as such.
No bright tunnel, she said, or dark light
just to meander through befogged faces
that look past you accusingly like collectors.

Their mother (why we were there)
had once danced with Loie Fuller.
On a publicity poster for her debut,
she posed on one foot as a white silkie.

Nearly a hundred, she could lift dumbbells
and do jumping jacks like a Rockette.
Though deaf, she told stories of dancing
in Vienna, Rome, Paris, Odessa.

At the kitchen sink after the meal
she'd dry each plate and stack it
before the next, leaving a clear place
behind each step she would take.

That way, I thought, death wouldn't find her
since there were no drips or traces.

A mile up in the clear blue sky
he swore the marble headstone was on point,
hawthorn blossoming white around the grave
a ballet corps before the dying swan.

A QUESTION OF MUSIC

There was a small clearing in the gorse where the man found rest. Sunlight on his face reassured him of his whereabouts in the labyrinthine topology of the region. A warm rock provided a seat. His memory recreated a dozen locales for the welcoming shadows, the cloud-studded sky, the still wind. What was unusual: when his head cocked slightly, there was music. He said the word to himself – *music* – because it wasn't certain. Cadence and melody, to be sure, and a kind of transport he associated with deep tonalities of great works, but what could he be hearing? It seemed celestial in expanse, rooting him to the spot and opening a vast space in his viscera. But when he looked round, there was no source. Mountainous terrain loomed over the valley, blocked east by a massive outcropping. The music ebbed to silence when it was all the stronger. Then its éclat blended most closely with the babble of a stream. Finally frustrated by the enigma, he retraced his descent. In the pasture beside his camp (which wasn't far from a monastery), a group of young girls practiced a dance. The precision of their gestures made him wonder. Approaching the party, he was surprised to see they were old women, crones, shrunken in body, yet capable of agile movement. When asked, one told him they were rehearsing a hymn. *But there is no sound*, he said. The woman pointed far off, toward the distant glen where he had been. Learning nothing more, he stayed until his curiosity grew unbearable. He returned to the spot below, to the same spectral melodic. That night and for several afterward, he could not sleep as his overheated brain tried to make sense of the phenomenon.

ARK OF MISFORTUNE

The woman in a red dress once told of a nephew who
played cello for the local symphony orchestra. He was
assistant director, in charge of funds. One day at an
auction he fell madly in love with a bust attributed to
Cellini. It was small and had a damaged ear. To make
matters worse, there was a dispute over authenticity. In
spite of its high cost, with great pathos he managed to
outbid everyone and for funds had to borrow from the
company account. Amidst loud clucking of tongues,
it went on display on the mantle over the backstage
fireplace. That week he unexpectedly cracked a
favorite bow. The next week, someone broke into the
orchestra storeroom and stole the kettledrum. As the
season progressed, and the house dwindled, it became
evident that the symphony would soon go bankrupt.
His colleagues pleaded with him to sell the Cellini, but
he was adamant. Then, at a gala, he bit into a lobster
dish and cracked two molars. In the pain of the dentist
chair, he realized what he had to do. The bust was sold,
the proceeds deposited, and life returned, as it were, to
normal. Soon after, he took a trip to the west coast, to
the museum that had bought the Cellini, to gaze again
upon his beloved. He read the curator's note, which
said how it had been made under the master's direction
(but not his hand.) Its label read, *Attributed to the school of
Cellini.*

THE ART OF FLOATING

We are born wet but water was never my element.

As a boy, I eschewed baths on principle
since a body purifies itself and is untainted
while the mind plots with poison.

Cajoling failed to bring a desired effect
and heightened threats nurtured a rebellious spirit:
 dives in mud below the spring house.

What saved the neighbours from a quarantine
was a small, unpretentious wooden contraption
my mother named my Portuguese man-of-war.

It floated but not in imitation of a sailing ship.
Why *man* was a name for a spoon of pine
was a question that left me confused.
I couldn't find a human being in it.

Nonetheless it raced rim to rim,
growing heavy and waterlogged
to sink right side down like a dead fish,
bobbing pathetically between top and tub.

In the time before the ballast took it
all pretend hands fell to their knees.
I imagined wild tribes of the Amazon
as their canoes circled for the kill.

Trade routes were printed in my mind
(practice for future work in importing),
mining colonies planted and defended.

That was life at sea, obeying law and fortune.

The small adventure persisted while soaped down
under a determined and abrasive washcloth

while I gave a Portuguese song
with words that poured from my mouth
in a guttural imitation of warm grog.

That didn't make the hull more seaworthy.
Often a capacity for greatness is served
in denial of the real facts about life.

In later years I emerged from the ritual bath
with fair knowledge of windspeed
and wave-form, but no love of the sea.

This came to a head when the *Lusitania*
hit a reef nearing the Cape of Good Hope.
Baba Lekker had been uncertain of travel.
In the end, the China trip was a bad deal.

I read what the newspapers reported.
A naval spokesman announced the ship
went down due to a waterlogged cargo,

thick bristled trunks of black mahogany
culled from African rain forests
unsalvageable, so heavy with the sea.

THE WATCH

The surface was glass. My father rowed.
The oars made fishtails as they fluted water.
Distant fishing boats trolled for
the moon that exerted a watery force.

On a backwater eddy of a mighty river.
The Saint Lawrence had coelacanths in its deep.
My father steered respecting their presence.
Their heavy gills lifted like oars to breathe.

Where we would beach receded as we neared.
The sublunary glow was silver. It flattened
the oars' tiny putsch which was insufficient
to lay siege to the silent tidal current.

When my sister let out intermittent cries
– dream or panic attack – progress went on paused.
Captain, O Captain, my father leaned aft to console
or snuff out the mutinous uproar.

Along with waves that lapped the gunwales
as they sought a new balance for the boat,
there was, I heard, an indistinct plop below,
a canister opening under pressure,
ordnance as the fuse ignites.

I imagined the *whosh* escaping
the scramble to void the energetic mess
that stained and would cause my mother
to recite her catalogue of reprimands.

The watch my father got for Guadalcanal
had slipped back into the birth element.

Flares drowned the bay under Marine assault.
Dead soldiers joined the tide's retreat.
The medics (like my father) performed triage
on corpses already pilfered for memorabilia.

There was a torn Jap flag in the cedar closet,
bullet holes rent the Rising Sun.
To touch the silken tatter felt shameful.
I would bury it under Army patches.

He leaned far astern, a fisher over water.
Soft sobs, smothered by waves.
They prefigured later shipping news,
mordant silence, my grandmother's disbelief.

Think of torpedoes, *kamikaze*, naval atrocities,
maimed sailors, bereft of any hope,
a future of internecine war,
but a single stifled cry sized that pity.

It came to signify the wreck of a man
his hours, a small prize, now drowned
in the seepage of oceans.

Years after, a gaudy gold watch,
hung disgracefully loose at the wrist.
Its Roman face, the colonist's,
bound to vanish too in seizing time.

THE PAINTER

Sunlight diffusing through a curtain.
It lived a flaccid, weightless existence,
and spread a gauzy blue, perfume
to spray air with marvellous flotsam.

Did I float too? It seemed so,
a compass needle on a magnetic sea.

There was brown. Brown was brusque.
Brown was the sound of my mother's voice.
It pulled back to ground, a wood poop deck.

Straight lines were most difficult.
Oil-thick, they liked to slither
around shapes and spread beyond limits.

They were like light but more recalcitrant.
And: had to land in the right number.

My hand, guided more by silence
than voice, eyes closed, I was blind.

There shouldn't be decisions to make.
Rules exist to subdue the mind:
my dilemma vis à vis brown.
It would be a recurrent life issue.

Bluer than ever, the diffusion was
a gulf, a sea, an aqueous mandate.
Though my mother was right she was wrong
the way *blue* would swallow her.

For now the ship was a blank relief.
It floated possessively on the charging
main. Someone was at the helm the way an artist is
who raced through patches of number four.

The ship, copied from the last *Esmeralda,* was
a Portuguese brig but an imperfect body. It didn't
like water that clung like an adherent
as if it repelled the element of survival.

The painting hung above the bed, unfinished.

That is the argument, stuck in the craw,
sea or craft, contained or container.
I left home one dark night knowing
unsaid words, like oil, calm waters
held tense in impulsive denial.

Bedtime prayers to that good ship:
dear Father, plug the runs in the color blue.

At shore where waves break stride,
a newly-deposited crop of jetsam,
empty crab shells litter the beach.

One whole summer I spent tossing live ones
back to a storm-swollen surf,
each brown, spidery set of lines dropped
forever into the incorrigible blue.

A NOTICE IN THE MAIL

I never meant to be an explorer.
At birth it was already old
to ask what land it would be
(to stretch the metaphor) without bearings,
beneath an august gaze of stars
that move with time across an open field.

Thus it seemed an errancy:
how the straight way was crooked
an ill wind made sorcery with life
no good word to turn ashes back to gold.

What looked suddenly near seemed
a mirage of untended projects,
yet when humility ought to be born
it was not. It was dire.

Crashes, forced retreats, servitude,
mislaid plans and bland timidity
did nothing to impart discretion,
most stiff-necked of all virtues.

Pooh-poohing a new interest in nature.
An artist friend who'd read
Paul Klee said I turned to wildflowers,
bound to a long, dry apprenticeship.

Writing took on a new form: long lists.
Actually an old habit, taught
to elaborate story lines and characters,
now articulated genus names and habitats.

The birdfeeder was a second diversion.
An owl patrolled the yard,
lauded a small flock that fed there,
so much that it needed to be removed.

When the starlings left, it saddened me
more than the impulse to produce,
but the latter was obediently accepted
as the iron hand inside the glove.

Nature abhors a vacancy.

As lists, a new plague, sickened thoughts
I became intent on the humdrum.
The stove remained impeccably clean.
Mail sorted, picture frames dusted.

Gods be even here. Words pinned above the laundry sink.

THE ICE FACTORY

The water like a glass curtain
as morning sunlight sprayed
prismatic mists that coloured the city.

Behind sat my grandfather, hands folded
at a folding card table. He played cribbage.
In the kitchen my grandmother at her stove,
the music of bake tins clanging.

It seemed then the real mystery
was how water stood straight up,
a file of spume as from a great leviathan
whose hunger pounced at the sky above
only to drop hypnotically to the roof.

Years later, fascinated, I read eye-
witness accounts of Ausable Falls.
Victims would faithfully follow
the water slow-motion to the rock bed,
excessive joy
was illicit as life's beauty.

The towering water spray was to be watched
because no one told me not to.
Perhaps the loss of agency
or volition calmed my thoughts
or perhaps it was access to the forbidden.

The pegs on the cribbage board had tips
white like thin columns of water.
Unlike the factory scene, they stayed upright.

My grandfather never hurried.
With graceful resignation the game ended.
Taking my hand, he led me to the park.

Sleight-of-hand was his métier.
Cards vanished, eggs pulled from behind ears, candied
fruit slices spread on the divan
all colors of the rainbow: magic.

Perhaps he'd made my real grandfather vanish into
the cold sea with the *Lusitania*.
The stories he told by my bedside
would be about lost children.
Happy endings added by my grandmother but
his voice soft like the ocean
rising to sky and becoming cloud.

Back from the park, I went to the window.
Water still fell to the plinth
in the time it takes angels to light.

I couldn't hear the talk behind me.
War news spewed from the domed Dumont
blending with my mother's silent sadness. So I
learned tears in the world are constant.

In uniform my father watched from the oak frame. At

times, a question appeared:
Will the water ever stop?
By this I must have meant, end.

Language brought an anxious fear
I didn't know then of the landing craft
that floundered at the beach near Iwo Jima, and

how the Japanese mortar shell found the
medics, who left the living behind.

Later, learning water was the universal solvent,
I knew why the Army
was never able to find his body.

My grandmother pulled me from the window.
She was afraid I was getting sick
but I was really the opposite (in some sense). I felt
looked at by the white cascade.

The zone where it turned to vapour
called my eye. In school I heard how
the sun sucks seawater up
to make a storm cloud, the sound
of which echoed the word *shroud* to me.

That evening my grandfather did tricks to
cheer me (I wasn't sad).

As I lay in bed, streetlights danced
across the ceiling, played by the rain.
It came from the factory roof
on runs on the route back from heaven.

The only trouble was it didn't fall
which made it soundless,
a mid-air flood held in suspension
while all the world beneath, dry as bone.

AT MID-LIFE

To paint the moon was my ambition,
in water like a Phoenician drum
not the moon in a pond, Japanese style
but teary, an over-brimming eye.

Banal, my artist friend said at dinner.
The French did it the last century.
On the street, the moon was just another lamp.
The idea died like a bit of roadkill.

Others introduced me to the abstract
where I've been ever since,
flat, critics say, without heart.

I was assuaged by the thought of destiny
since even a mediocre one was justice.
It took me back into boyhood books
with stories of divine disfavour:
to be one with the misaligned.

One winter I lived on Nantucket.
The house my daughter rented was tiny,
my room a bare closet. I was happy.

On a night walk, I'd wandered off.
How to get lost on a postage-stamp island?
The circles retraced were untrue.
They bent at the ends like backs of chairs.

To forestall frostbite, I burrowed in sand.
It was overcast. The surf was close.
I drifted with waves, in and out of shore.

I was ice, I was flotsam, a door broken
from a loose lobster trap, old piling,
rubber tubes, a marooned harbour porpoise.

To sleep while death passes over.
That blessing.

Just at dawn the old moon woke me,
a grain of sand blurred my vision
or tears did. Seagulls wheeled above my eyes.

I threw the paintbox in the surf, watching
it float fatefully toward Ireland.

Years that followed produced equanimity.
I accepted the poverty of work, with no thought
to lessen it. Wisdom escaped possession.

Where I'd settled far out west
suited a new temper, listless withdrawal
as anonymity wrapped itself around me.

Cowhand, lumberjack, jack
of all trades, grafter, school teacher.
The menial opened its doors,
with no strings attached.

Under a sky by the Great Salt Lake
I watched clouds scud to one corner
where they huddled in disdain of their role.

The sign I had sought was like that.
As I packed, an ancient letter
forwarded from a *poste restant* floated up:
an invitation to show at OK Harris.

Frenetic contingency undid my anchor,
stalling great temptation. I succumbed.

Outside after the opening, the city
put on a celestial wetness. The moon
stood in a puddle wearing a serape.

You must paint, my daughter said.
Old work had made my name.
A passerby heard it in French – *passé*.

I returned to a garret on the island.
A sea glass collection stood in a jar.
The sketchbook lay open, a blank page.

Are we not the edge of things
like old maps of earth, about to drop off?
It seemed I'd fallen into a repetition
serially washing hands to kill germs.

The ocean that day was grey with fog.
Any hopes I had were undistinguished.

The moon was a disc on the tidal pool,
a flat nothing that shaded
an iridescent pearl swimming in my eye.

THE DOUBLE

In the faded photo, my aunt holds
the other one, who looks urgently into
the camera, a Brownie Hawkeye, an inheritance.
Almost out of focus, my mother kneels beside.
Can she feel the misbelonging
that would stalk life for me?

These legacies are undoubtedly framed
by vagaries from before birth.

In her depression, she took to needlepoint.
The calming effect issued in many samplers.

Schroon Lake (in the background) was
their refuge from war news.
The beach was a borrowed stripe of rock
the shape of a flatiron.
The rule was shoes in the water.

Memory is like a canteen
with a long invisible straw
to suck sediment from the bottom.

Afternoons we would lie on the dock
and watch clouds take shapes
of the beings that formed them.
Goats were favorites because of the horns.

Pareidolia is the term for seeing forms
where they don't exist. My mother, a victim.

My cousin, the other one, was contrary.
Whatever I named, he said the opposite.
What is the opposite of a whale?

After his Air Force rescue mission crashed
I felt remorse at believing he'd stolen
my identity when it was never mine.
By which I mean it didn't want to be seized.

The matter of the double grew obsessive.
On summer vacation once I saw him
standing by my car. We stared.
Another time, some rowdy Canadians asked

if I was X, who was the image of me.
He lived in the Gaspé and did trapping.

Was I one half of a twin, the other half dead,
or was it an appalling diversion to a role
of a placid life, settled by habit?

Wisteria blossoms trembled, weak ones
dropped, in the photo, onto the playpen.
He knew numbers already, a prescience
that would become a radiologist.

Fear of the *doppelgänger*, my therapist said,
came from survival guilt,
one twin having died before the other was born.

Once, in a revolving door, an image
of a man showed his haughty character,
jaunty fedora, tasteless jacket.
I was shocked to see it was my reflection.
Apparently I didn't know myself.

I would lie foetal on the leather couch.
Street shadows made nameless ciphers
that tried to spell Persian words on the ceiling.

The feeling of a solitude that wasn't real
because the second was somewhere lurking
severely compromised my well-being.
Was there a talisman to break the spell?

When I walked out, clouds had departed.
Above the skyscrapers, stars sprinkled light
to cool my brain, heated from
burning the family tree, limb by limb.

A taxi came to take me home.
The cabby watched my eyes read the ID,
a long Slavic name and a date
of birth the same as mine.

I tipped dangerously. He thanked me.
Driving off, he waved and smiled,
it's not really me. My brother is a twin.

VEIL

I'm not much of a moon person.
A ship can't be steered by the moon.
The eye needs a fixed point
not a fickle one that waxes and wanes.

The huntress is caught in the net
of her own making, the old woman said.
Silence on the park bench burrowed under
wisteria, me on the other end.

She's a prisoner. There she keeps time that
she unweaves so it won't run out. Silence
again. You missed the last bus. Her last
words seemed meant for me.

In her glasses were two moons.
They glared like headlights that froze me a
target dead-centre in the road.

Her voice grew hazy and overcast. Once
the moon hunted the ocean. Its
whiteness was pure and loved by a
certain woman. I was she.

The very next day it was gone.
I knew grief deeper than
the moon's fullness of tears.

I came to honour mathematics, she added:
love divided by death has no remainder.

Do you believe in ghosts?
She pointed at the moon, already setting
behind the trees' limbs. It's phantom.
It's a lost body, its whiteness is no
natural thing.

Years later, there was a full lunar eclipse.
Suddenly the moon was a red ball in 3-D,
not a bright thin plate.

The old woman's words came back. I'd
had to walk home that night.
The moon's surface had the glare
of a jealous lover, stronger dead
than the beautiful woman in life.

The tears (fear? joy?) made lines
as they ran down my face,
tracing that selfsame figure
that came moments before my sleep.

I was leery of prophets who spy
a delivery date in the future.

Another moon, another bench (empty)
years after, I on a silent watch, brimming
as the old woman's words resounded,
this time with prescience.

My wife had ended life in flames (literally).
The sky was white-hot, empty
of heart, a cruel appetite
to turn everything else to ashes.

Sadness wandered through the ruins
aimless as low ground fog.
Since my vision was veiled
and powerless, I saw nothing.

Nothing.

I stood up, blind.
It was that way for some time.

When I could again see, the moon
drifted above, a ghost ship at sea.
But I was not the same.

The silence was gone. I could speak.

THE SLIDE

Even the word *height* causes anxiety.
It started with a dive, to speak factually.
In water, I mean.

I was seated alone on the top of
'the tallest water slide in the State of Texas.'
At bottom was a shallow pool
which was barely visible below.

Whose hands buoyed me
in the brine, I can't recall.
Were they rough or smooth
or just wet skin, or skin at all?

Angels, I imagine, move with arms
outstretched like mothers who carry.

Whose hands? one asks
only after being saved, *if...*
My father, beached at Guadalcanal
never found the right question.

Once on a flight a seatmate said,
seven miles down to the big splash.
The Challenger crew had time
enough to think that matter through.

I ended west in another life
writing music for the movies, bad ones.
Silence was just another way to fill
a treble clef with deadbeat drone.

The cabin I rented stood on a
cul de sac of a steep mountain road.
Eagles screamed in rapture of flight.
Rain clouds draped a valley below.
A bowl of oak galls stood on the desk.

My nephew came to live with me.
He didn't share my view on water.
There was a *trompe l'œil* he painted
of a tranquil lake on the kitchen wall.

Though he was depressive
my phobias were entertainment.
He went on to live an artist's life
charming clients with life-sized deceptions.

I had contracted a peculiar deafness.
It had a name I don't know –
a person can hear only human voices
spoken aloud to him. Why height is
a cause is a medical mystery.

Heaven must suffer a gravitas
that lengthens shadows before their time
or when an anchor drops sighingly at sea.

Little as it was, I had work no more.
In St. Louis, I drove a rogue cab
and let poverty close in on me.

Destiny has a different ring when
you're poor. It's an iron cage.

One evening I drove into the river.
(My night vision was nonexistent.)
In hospital, the nurses were humming
a haunting melody. They said
I'd arrived on the ambulance, singing.

This story has a happy ending.
The fickle hand of fortune, a banal image,
played a part. My drowning song
was an instant success on the radio.
It made what they call the hit parade.

Sadly, fears like mine are not cured.
But as with other spiteful things,
their weight may well equal gold.

SUNDAY WALK

Parallel was a favorite word of mine.
It rivalled *biped* and *gnomic*
because it made me feel flush with science.

That someone decided parallels should never meet
was a strain on my mental life.

They were almost everywhere I looked:
twin brows of a ship's wake,
lines of flight of gulls aloft
mirror image of clouds on salt spray
lovers looking in opposite directions.

Present circumstances dictated the rule,
red line must lag behind green line.
If they touch, someone said, *c'est le fin*.

That day I aimed to disprove geometry
as I walked on creosote ties between tracks.
The steel rails gamely stretched
to infinity where red and green blotted together.

A nurse came running. An orderly
pounded my chest as if I owed money.

That day (I remember) was clear and clairvoyant.
My mind had dispelled all the disjunctions
that a life haplessly provides.

(My cousin had said on a sphere's surface,
no parallels exist. Everything crosses.
There is no tranquillity
because no choices have to be made.)

I wore boots. Each step was a mile.
I walked a bed of clinkers, past old stone walls
steam-scorched by the engine heat,
a dead ocelot, broken beer bottles
cigarette butts (hundreds), a baseball cap,
a commuter's train schedule.

Someone else walked with me besides
my shadow, a third who remained apart
wanting to talk from *there*.

Admiral Byrd (I read) had a similar experience
during the expedition to the North Pole.
Perhaps the mind plays tricks, or God – or death.

True, the heat had gone to my head,
like a moth to the flame.
Are you unhappy? the other asked.

A trailer to the conversation
that appeared when opening my journal.
Are you writing? he repeated.
The coast never seemed farther away.

Tell me your name, I said. A pause of restraint.
You know it isn't allowed, he said.
Another mile: *We are different,* he said.
You want us to be the same but I'm not.

A hot wind braised my temples. The tracks
were a broken-down staircase leading south.
You mustn't disdain the truth, he was saying,
then silence, the copper taste of fear,
a long deep chasm into which we strode.

Are you alone? The voice sounded like hope
squashed inside Pandora's box. Actually,
it was just a scratch in my throat.

The orderly ended his violence in a flourish
that announced truce on the battlefield.
The screen showed lines that were parallel again.
He cheerfully transcribed notes into my clipboard.

The gaiety in the room was explosive.
Laws of geometry were forgiving and
in the freedom I imagined the completion of
the novel stowed in the top desk drawer.

The doctor shook my hand and pronounced
I'd soon feel again like a new man.

The words seemed deeply fraudulent
but come evening I was at my typewriter.

Lines appeared, to my relief, evenly one by one,
chasing each other down the page.

If only on the bland surface, they respected
the perpetual distance that held them apart.

A new proof: one plus one equals one.

THE MOTTLED PORTION

I saved this one for last.

Love is a perquisite to my story.
It came in drips and left in droves.
It was brief, it was long
like snow sighing over branches
the air full of secrets
down cliff-side to the lake
to the deepenings themselves
the edge of night where it waits.

There was a room.
I understand why this is always so
if only as an stale idiom.

We sat in the kitchen cracking chestnuts.
Wine from old-world root-stock
whose skins drop languidly with the pulp
in glasses all the way from China.
Beeswax candle spills onto the table.

I didn't know the language.
How do words hold onto things?
When does *light* really become something?

What is a shibboleth?

Her look fell onto me and stained
the morning news like pollen from wisteria.

Perhaps words then came from roots
beyond my farthest travels
invisible save to tiny vague animals
that scurry from the hazards.
(There are as many as unplayed desires.)

Why have I come here? I asked her.
I am so easily crushed.

Children gathered outside silent, bewildered.
News of love had brought tears
which they thought the Emperor would wipe away.

Perhaps they were tears of betrayal,
suchlike are often found together with love.
Bitter, sweet, we did not love one another
as Tristan and Iseult did.
How much simpler if we had.

She watched rain wet the studio roof.
Waiting coiled inside her, waiting for me
to say which rule to obey.

There were no laws of seduction.

My brother who died young said
a ship passes, there is the wake and some spray,
and then it disappears.

It isn't quite true. While the mark
in water is temporal, memory persists.
I mean it glorifies
the body removed, the cave empty:
that is the revelation itself.

There then were omens. [*Omen*,
From *oiomai*, I believe, related to
audire, to hear.]

Phone dead on the other end,
unmailed letters, unopened letters,
letters to me that weren't for me,
lists that made no sense
[massage oil roses anise candy]
bedclothes in the washing machine
car keys strangely displaced.

But I meander. Proof didn't exist.
One day the whole thing fell apart
like a crossword puzzle
when one word unlocks the deal,
a small word like the indefinite article.

It was the sense that most demoralizes.
Taste.
Not a good password.

That's how it happened; hope was remade.
The power of the unexplained.

To make a deal with the devil
is not a crime but love's story.

Genuflect.
What a beautiful word.

GHOST BROTHER

When my brother came back from war
he was a ghost. I'd planted castor beans
in my mother's tiny victory garden.
Green sprouts dared the last April snow.

He haunted the living room since I moved
into a bedroom that had been his.

I was like you once, he whispered one night,
in love with rich things. That is life.

We were on hands and knees searching
for the bag of Army patches
that held the battle-worn Japanese flag
with real bullet holes through the Rising Sun.
It was from a beachhead the Marines lost.

What did you learn from service? I asked him.
He looked startled. (He was a phantom.)
Luck deserts you in little pieces.
Missed deadlines, wrong numbers, bounced checks.
Then there is Schadenfreude:
I hoped my bunkmate would get shot.

I will visit the cemetery, I assured him.
There is none since I was buried
at sea, with the good word wanting.

Then I'll stand in front of a wall and scream
curses as Gandhi did during the salt tax march.
His enemies took him to have gone mad.

Perhaps reading from the Homeric Odes
would be more compliant, he replied.

I'd recently found work as a printer's devil.
Words were rolled up in dust balls
under the piano stool and by the ottoman,
glint, pylon, and *savant* were among
the favorites of his, but inertia has
a life of its own (or rather, doesn't)
where there was the pinochle table.

Intimacy was his indifference
as if he floated above both our lives
watching the flare-ups untouched.
It lent a vivacity to my thoughts that
out of habit were suppressed.

Would you do it all again? I asked.
Light poured through the jalousies
making a checkerboard on the card table.
It divided the silence into yesses and nos.

The gap was long and I felt constrained
to speak again. *I mean, have you regrets?*

Forgiveness precedes judgment
like a mother who punishes a naughty child.

So it must have been I felt his gaze on me
and how in the remainder, which was all,
we shared without speaking another word.
It seemed like a puzzle.

I cleaned up and walked outside.
The city, its highways and storefronts,
gleamed with a million lights.
The shadows were deep with couples
who walked arm in arm through them.

By the dock were the big ships.
Among them, the *Aurelia*, once impounded
for troop transport, my father among them.
Then, the harbor, and beyond, the ocean, where
questions of faith were answered.

There was the carnage of the invisible,
the worst kind.

I watched.

High up at the railing, the old man stood
with a spyglass, gazing without seeing.
It was myself on deck, not knowing
I was on view.

It was tremendous.

As the night was young, I stopped at a
sedate neighborhood bar called Jimmy's.

THE FALLACY OF MISPLACED EMPHASIS

There were constantly the stars. When the unshuttered
feeling arose, I walked outside. My hopes were off the
mark, only entropy prospered. Was insincerity the deck
that been dealt against me? Life seemed vacuous. Faces
were fewer to count as a review progressed, trial of my
disdain, as friends would part before being done with
them. The feeling brought to mind a boyhood game called
Sardines, when isolation—being among the last to get it—
gave an incomprehensible foretaste of then-remote old age.
Inevitably came the time when I was the last man standing,
absolutely alone. The rest were hidden in safe company.
That was the idea. I had lost. But I had 'won' fame. The
difficult irony of quotation marks. More so, their embrace
of life. Outside whirled the galaxies, blinking on, blinking
off, distant, impossibly close. The contradiction was
calming. The dull inconstancy retreated inside, home on
the home planet.

THE HIT

Was it a birthday?
Tante Faiga lit the candle,
the only one. The *shamas*.

The whiteness of the carrot cake
more than the album
always holds some secret force,
a magic potion consumed to repair the past.

In the picture of who was there,
Simonides, host of the fiesta, tell
whether they were to receive mercy
or sorrow, or if you know a difference.

My cousin once gave me a present
wrapped in a big box. Inside,
one smaller and inside that...
As they say, turtles all the way down. The
smallest contained a single baseball. I was not
happy with his conjuring.
Joy had struck out mightily.

In the secretness of the neutral, credit
colours in numbered patches
to hide the lines, forbidden to cross – there
the subject stands, as is said, out – to worship
in the blue surround
the brig, portrayed as dying Icarus.

Light battered the blinds not
because it was bright but
because it was hostile.

Before Tante Faiga cut the cake she
drew channels for the portions. (Can
you slice one length-wise?)
They were like guide lines sunk beneath blue
oil paint which meandered years scouting for
oases in the picture frame while the marine
terms lost meaning while ideals became
idolatry.

Baseballs too had lines,
seams, really, which came into view
when a pitch stood still in mid-air,
a simple object that met the bat's
irresistible force with abandon.

But please don't cry.

That, after the low parabolic line drive –
barely suspending gravity – whacked
the fielder's mitt, evading the grandstand.
That was my closest brush with heroism.

All lines lead from somewhere
in response, a mine of random solitude
that refuses to provide shelter. I took to
a career in publicity for compensation.
My therapist, a young man, had put it thus.
Now all lines ineluctably lead there.

To end up a publicist is as discomfiting
as a blind sailor at the helm.
Thus I could do no harm swabbing
the deck down when needed.

I walked outside after my session.
Rain fell from a lowering sky.
Faust and the devil, my therapist said,
enjoyed a working relation.

Please don't cry.

CAMP SHELBY

All the houses were the same.

Distance would remain a life problem
almost powdery to the touch.
In this regard it was not unlike ageing.

The lines were the same because of the Army.
Streets, water mains, pitch of the roofs.
Distinction was rationed, not for equality's sake
but in fear of disobeying a command.

If I took a step out and wanted
to come back to the same place,
any house would do: infancy of reason.
There was terror in not being right.

The first time is the time
of inexperience, 'a flashbulb memory'.

The woman, a mother not my own,
had hands of infinite mercy.
With her I was put back in the same house,
where Edith Piaf sang on the radio.

Angels:
their hands are half-sheathed in cookie dough.

Later it was the same way with words.
Angels, I mean, are needed to make sense
of the filament of thought in the brain.
Windows had to be unshuttered,
light let in to bleach the molecules.

My father told me, *If you go out,*
we are number one three two:
how I found out numbers don't work.

My father spoke little and not easily.
Crossword puzzles lay on waiting room tables.
He didn't believe in angels.
When the landing boat was breached,
any trace of his words was lost.
Water makes ink run all over.

Once I woke in recovery from a near-drowning.
The beds all looked like the other.
Ether erased the differences.
To mark where my bed ended
and the abyss began, a railing
had been erected for safe-keeping.

An orderly hummed *La vie en rose.*
Hold me close and hold me tight.

The sunlight had a familiar slant to it
as when the movie turns to credits.

I was feeling it wasn't the first time
because the staid ending was to dissolve
and leave my mouth with a metallic taste.

The Piaf song came to a final refrain.
When you speak, angels sing from above.

The steel railing was cool to my forehead.

The sunset, red like the blood-red surf, raged
against normalcy, as when an avenging sword
passes over a house asleep, and dreams
scatter like ants from an overturned stone.

THE BLINDNESS BEFORE FRIENDS

A split second before was more normal
than the explosion
the stone launched, suspended mid-air
time about to rocket off in two directions.

In every life, an empty frame,
past and future, one brother grasping
the other's heel, before separation.

Normal is unclear in intent to this day,
then running home crying strange words.
It doesn't feel like me anymore.
Enough to make a mother die.

The sight that had been there was gone.
When the doctor lifted a sharp instrument
a scream from my mouth dropped it to the floor.

There was no escape from the current of
transcendent heredity.

Baptism in my case was irrelevant.
From my loins would spring a line
of Cyclopes, looming one-eyed beings
in a hostile binocular world.

My young friend (before the accident)
was punished and outlawed forever.
His claim: he'd been free of sin.

My son (mine from a brief liaison)
suffered vision without a right eye.
Portraits he painted were designed to work
in profile as if whispered in your ear
to be not judged by the visual lack.

Mister Horus One-Eye sees the world
from the wings, synaptic change.

My mentor was that, a black patch
menaced one eye while the good eye
looked through you to the bones
as it mounted experimentally the heights above.

In his art the pen line was a rift.
Reverse fields, white for black,
and the sheet of paper seen from above
evolves into some further triumph.
From below, it is white, crisscrossed
by lines that divide adjoining planes.

Paintings from his studio followed you
around the corner and ended up where
yes and no were stuck together, at the start.
People paid handsomely for his imbroglios.

My own career (to use a euphemism)
was unremarkably bland.
One reason was because the affected eye
wasn't blinded, just scratched,
as if the world now screamed through
the rifts to become displaced pixels,
no simple hatred, no black ink,
no second sight of a Tiresias.

The sun was shining through the original
darkness. Actually it was the examination
lamp, blinding the good eye. Put
the blood-soaked rag over it, stop the light.

The doctor, who had studied for psychiatry,
said, *Nothing happens by accident*.
An observation on how to live like an adult
designed to trigger my survivor guilt.

Did it mean my mother saw her destiny
the impossible night the tree rammed her car?

On the crowded sidewalk, people watched
as I was funnelled into an ambulance.
The world now flat, void of depth, drove by.

There would be dreams of space truncated
so my finger could touch objects a mile off
a life beat its way toward me, unshielded.

The implication, there whenever I blinked.
It was a puzzle. It was a cliché.

DEPARTURE

Tunnel vision.
I didn't have the word
so there was a hole for it

into which she fell.
My grandmother receded without distance.
It prefigured being enfolded by her apron
after I came from the funeral.

That sinkhole opens whenever I look
sidewise out of a car's rear window.

Exiled from vision, she came truer
to memory, a silk nightgown
that would press against my temple
to rub away all vanities.
She was the first one added to my map.

No word could have saved me
from wandering the outside shore
in the deceit of a crab's progress.

This, the story of a crime against the mother.
I was made to eat the pomegranate seed.
Afterwards, my father's car never slowed
its hellish movement forward
while abandoned, my grandmother blighted all things
living within her reach.

The map was of the tunnel.
There was no light in it.
I clawed my way out every few months.

Back on the surface, roses in bloom
form a crown for the lintel.
Ask yourself, made to eat how?

It must have been she knew the word.
My sister, who wasn't in the car,
said it was to abolish seduction.

The dementia, she meant.

I could never visit her bedlam.

She would cry across the room, *Yingle*.
The eyes look back through layers,
concave and vexed, of old glass,
to advance a conspiracy. In whose name?

Though not part of the story, my sister
became a pushpin on my map
placed near the Cape of Good Hope
where the mouth of the tunnel was.

I imagined a pickling wind
that cut through stone statues
a garden where she and her midshipman
would walk forever,
unfazed by our mother's grief.

She was a poor daughter.
Sour seed, stunted trees, rotted corn.

The graveside procession stalled
when the hearse overheated
some distance into the Battery Tunnel.

Oily white steam enrobed the vehicle,
an act of magical bereavement.

You stay down below, her voice spoke.
For the devil's share: monkshood and flax,
make them flower. My victory.

THE DANCE

It was the last dance.
Idle at the keyboard, a gaunt
piano hire shuffled his few sheets of music.

My aunt was swaying her head
to the beat, so holding her waist
brought my whole body into motion.

We were alone on the oak parquet
facing the end
which I saw open beneath our feet,
a pool that held my sister
even as my mother expired in delivery
of her stillborn soul.

Waters that break too early.

Yingle, please don't cry.

Later, unpacking in my room
an impulse to test the desk drawer.
There, my sabotaged novel, papers
limp and curled at the edges.

The thought came that mothers
name their sons in secret
who in turn are born into debt
until they find how to say it.

Mine was repaid many times
with strangers who adapted me
to their needs and fears.

At the balcony, the typescript lay open.
Outside the cool evening
made the cicadas' drone less frantic.
A lone lawnmower reasserted its rights
to publicity.
Stars were partly occluded by high mist.

I tried. I shunned self-slander.

The pure gravity of existence
weighted me to the chair.

The dance floor scene floated
in conspiracy with my calm,
details for which scripted a strange font.

An army chest in the closet
held bundles of onionskin letters
each stamped with the censor's mark.
The signature was her husband's
illegible scribble, coded like the name
of an unknown soldier.

The moral history that wasn't.

At the dance, after all, wasn't it she,
come like Odysseus' mother
wanting blood?

It was already said
somewhere in the marrow of the book,
the letters that named the spell.

The thought, deeply fraudulent,
disturbed the beauty of the night.

Existence will not stop until
it comes to beauty.
My resolve was broken.
The story would find another way to end.

The earth had returned to imperfect sleep.

I want to offer my thanks to Todd Swift, BSPG publisher and the editorial staff, ESPECIALLY Alex, Cate, Edwin and Amira, without whose support and encouragement this project would not have come to fruition.